The Little Book of Love

from the Chequamegon Bay and beyond

The Little Book of Love from the Chequamegon Bay and Beyond

Printed by SmartPress
Book Design: Annette Flaig
Book Advice: CopyThat
Partially funded by a Thrivent Action Team grant
ISBN: 978-0-9644736-8-3

To receive more copies of this book send
$6.00 plus $2.00 for shipping and handling.
Mail to:
The Little Book of Love
P.O. Box 114
Washburn, WI 54891
Make checks payable to Nancy Hanson.

Dedicated to those who simply want to live their authentic lives.

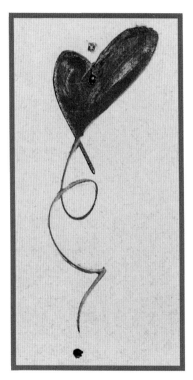

Karen Maki

Welcome to The Little Book of Love

If you are transgender or non-binary, or know someone who is, this book is for you.

This is a book of messages from parents, grandparents, and others who love you.

Older transgender and non-binary people have told us how much they wish they had a little book of love when they were growing up.

There is a ton of love out there for you. And, love always survives hate. Sometimes other people say things because they don't know any better. Someday they will see the beauty in everyone, each of us.

Until then, we need to remind ourselves of our dignity, value, and worth. May this book help you feel whole, just as you are.

Rev. Nancy Hanson and Annette Flaig

Emma

2

Choose to be HAPPY !

We love you to the

moon and back

Puppa and Nana

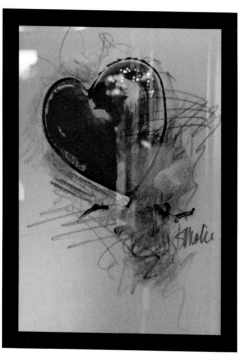

Karen Maki

You don't get between a Mama Bear and her cubs! GRRRRR!

Kate

Jay Pond

Someone loves you.

We love you.

We love all of your perfections.

We love all of your

imperfections.

We love you no matter what.

Mom & Dad in Corny

Ruby

Being your true self
takes so much courage.
At times it will feel lonely,
but know there are so many
people ready to accept you as
you are. You are worthy of
love and the life you desire.
You are valid and valued.

Mom

Joni Chapman

Change can be good
but only change for you.
Never change because
someone wants you to.
Be who YOU are and
remember you are amazing,
beautiful, and loved, so
never stop being you.

Dorian, age 15

Annette Flaig

You are, quite simply, loved. No matter the lies you hear or the lies you think — because your brain may lie to you from time to time — you are you, unique, loved.

Your 16-year-old friend

Kathryn

Depending on your mood:
With eyes closed and
a hand over your heart,
take three deep breaths.
Let kindness and love
enter deeply.
Picture unkind words
sliding off of you.
You are loved!
Or chant:
"I'm rubber, you're glue,
what you say bounces off me
and sticks to you."

A Mom

I don't see myself as a
transgender person. I just see
myself as a woman.
What I wish for everyone is to
have a church and home community
that accepts you.
I have this and it's priceless.

Carri (age 80) in Port Wing, WI

The only expert on you is
YOU.
Honestly, you're the only expert, even
among the people who know you the
best and love you the most. Give
yourself the gift of trusting
yourself - the expert!

Carver

Annette Flaig

When it gets hard and you feel all wrong, remember that you are enough, you are so loved, and you are important. Be brave when you can, and let the people who love you more than the sun and stars hold you up when you need it.

Love, Mama

Cindi Orley

Love is all around us. We have to have faith that it's there. Some people love us who are not good at showing it, so you have to ask for a hug or a talk or a walk. Feel the ground beneath your feet, see the big sky, nature all around you. Breathe it in. You will feel it.

Kate

G. Scott Hanson

You are worthy of love,
just the way you are.
Everything about you
is worthy of love.

Lucas in Ashland, WI

It is never too late to be
yourself. There's no
rush. Everybody's
timeline is different,
just as everyone's
journey is different.
Take a deep breath,and
trust that everything will
be just fine.

Lucas in Ashland, WI

Vivian

You are made of love
and are beautiful.
Yes, you!

You may not believe that, but it's
true. We don't believe it because we
believe what others have said to us
and about us. What others say
doesn't change the truth.
Not only are you made of love,
you are lovable, loved and loving!
Someday I hope you know this
beyond any shadow of a doubt!

Mom, Stone Lake, WI

G. Scott Hanson

You were you before you knew how
to express that you are trans.
You are still you now that you can
tell us you are trans.
We loved you before and we love
you now. For us nothing has
changed- except now we get to love
a part of you we didn't even know
about before. This part of you
awes us with the insight, courage,
and determination you found to
tell us who you really are at
such a young age.

Grandpa

Annette Flaig

Who you are is valid, and valued, and deserving of love. You deserve self-love, and you deserve romantic love if that is what you wish. You deserve the love that is found in lifelong friendships, and you deserve the safety that parental love offers, no matter how old we get. You deserve the anonymous love of strangers who fight for others' rights and ability to exist as they are. You deserve it all.

J in Ashland

Karen Maki

Your genuine Self may
challenge other people's
narrow ideas of what is possible,
but that is their limitation,
not yours.
The world only benefits from
your authentic self-expression,
expanding and celebrating all of
what it can mean to be human.
Please know in every cell
that your deep essence is
good, true, and beautiful.

Yarrow

Cows and Strawberries

Beverly

A college-bound 18-year-old submitted *Cows and Strawberries* for this book. The Chequamegon Bay area is known for its apples and berries. Wisconsin is known for its cow's milk cheese.

We cannot control other people's opinions on art, berries, cows, or anything else, but we can control what and who we read. The artists and authors in this book greatly love their friends, children, and grandchildren.

Let's all take more control over the images and messages we give ourselves. Maybe we need to view and read this little book every day for a while until we know at least some of the phrases by heart.

A huge shout of thanks to all who made *The Little Book of Love* possible. People of all ages contributed. Graphic artist Annette Flaig has made my dream come true.

With much love,
Nancy Hanson

Why This Book Now?
To Family and Friends

Members leave faith communities due to how LGBTQ+ people are treated. One of my closest friends feels spiritually wounded every time he goes to the church his grandchildren attend.

Some have created issues about what it means to be transgender and non-binary. Our friends and family members will hear hurtful and untrue messages.

Instead, let's continue to offer love, acceptance, and support. Now is the time to do one's own research. Now is the time to get to know at least one person who is trans or non-binary.

As long as wounding continues, we need words of love and kindness.

Rev. Mark Ricker sent more quotes:

You don't need a reason to be kind.
Mark in Appalachia, VA

We go through life.
We shed our skins.
We become ourselves.
Patti Smith

Let your words heal and not wound.
Mark

Did I offer peace today?
Did I bring a smile to someone's face?
Did I say words of healing?
Did I let go of my anger and resentment?
Did I forgive?
Did I love?
These are the real questions.
Henri Nouwen

Walk away from people who put you down.
Walk away from fights that will never be resolved.
Walk away from trying to please people
who will never see your worth.
The more you walk away from things
that poison your soul,
the healthier you will be.
Paulo Coelho, author of The Alchemist

Resources

Websites

genderspectrum.org • meditations@cac.org
pflag.org • thetrevorproject.org
transkidspurplerainbow.org
transmissionministry.com

Books

Transforming-The Bible & Lives of Transgender Christians by Austin Hartke, updated in 2023.
Raising Kids beyond the Binary: Celebrating God's Transgender and Gender-Diverse Children (2023) by Jamie Bruesehoff, Foreword by Sarah McBride.

People

Go to pflagwashburn.org to find ways to connect with other Chequamegon Bay area like-minded people. PFLAG is creating a caring, just, and affirming world for LGBTQ+ people and those who love them. Annette really loves her inclusive First Lutheran Church in Port Wing, WI. Nancy suggests reconcilingworks.org to find LGBTQ+ friendly churches including Chequamegon Bay area ELCA churches such as Messiah in Washburn, Bethesda in Bayfield, and Immanuel in Cornucopia, Wisconsin.

Call

877-565-8860 Trans Lifeline or
The Trevor Lifeline at 866-488-7386.